W9-CXN-284

# ELEVATE!

## JIM MCLAUGHLIN

ELEVATE

# JIM MCLAUGHLIN
## EXECUTIVE COACH

ELEVATE

ELEVATE

## Dedication

To my wife Peg, the woman who consented to
live life with me and elevated who I could
become in the process.

ELEVATE

ELEVATE

# Introduction.

*"I was actually lifted from nothingness to human life." Helen Keller*

These words from Helen Keller describe the moment she grasped the power of language, when she felt the presence of another mind: her teacher, Anne Sullivan. She was elevated from being, in her words, like an unconscious clod of earth.

It is in transformative moments like these we can suddenly see our worlds and our lives in a new way. Often, in a way that inspires or empowers us to make more of ourselves, more of our lives, and more of the world in which we live.

It is moments like these that I seek, that I work to create and co-create with the people in my life. It has become an elemental component of my life's work.

To paraphrase Einstein, the problems we face today cannot be solved at the level of thinking at which they were created. We must elevate our thinking, our language, our way of being.

This book is a collection of words and language that, it is my hope, will affect you in this way: to elevate you and the way you live your life, for the benefit of us all.

ELEVATE

The cave you fear to enter holds
the treasure you seek.

Joseph Campbell

ELEVATE

ELEVATE

I am not a product of my circumstances. I am a product of my decisions.

Stephen Covey

ELEVATE

ELEVATE

When I let go of what I am, I become what I might be.

Lao Tzu

ELEVATE

ELEVATE

## WHAT'S BEYOND YOUR COMFORT ZONE?

It really takes something to be in business, and sometimes it takes a lot. At the very least it takes courage, confidence, persistence and focus, and I'm sure you've heard many times it often requires you to get outside your comfort zone. But what does that really mean? It can mean facing your fears, but no one is at their best when they're facing their fears. Consider this. Consider that when you're at the edge of your comfort zone, it's simply that what's in front of you is unfamiliar. What's behind you is familiar. It may not be even that comfortable, but it's familiar so it seems comfortable. Instead try this. When you're looking out into the unfamiliar, be curious about it. Let your vision and your goals be your road map and move forward with curiosity and explore with confidence.

ELEVATE

Patience and perseverance have a magical effect before which difficulties disappear and obstacles vanish.

John Quincy Adams

ELEVATE

ELEVATE

If you're going through hell, keep going.

Winston Churchill

ELEVATE

ELEVATE

...I would like to beg you dear Sir, as well as I can, to have patience with everything unresolved in your heart and to try to love the questions themselves as if they were locked rooms or books written in a very foreign language. Don't search for the answers, which could not be given to you now, because you would not be able to live them. And the point is to live everything. Live the questions now. Perhaps then, someday far in the future, you will gradually, without even noticing it, live your way into the answer.

Rainer Maria Rilke

ELEVATE

Do or do not. There is no try.

Yoda

ELEVATE

ELEVATE

Strive not to be a success, but rather to be of value.

Albert Einstein

ELEVATE

ELEVATE

## TWO WAYS OF LIVING: SURVIVAL AND CONTRIBUTION

So, as part of an assignment, I'm pondering answers to these questions:

What is my life about?
What am I giving myself to?

...and out of the shadows of my mind comes this: "Survival."

Wow. That's not good. Survival is important, of course, but not very inspiring. Imagine someone greets you with, "How's it going?"

If you answer with "I'm surviving," you're likely to get a Stuart Smalley reply or a recommendation for a self-help book. Maybe both.

So, on I ponder, and then comes "Contribution."

Okay, that's better. I like contribution. In fact, I think contribution is part of our design, just like survival is. It may even be essential to our survival, like breathing.

Here's my logic. Over the years, I have heard many people say, "I just want to make a difference," or "I want to leave a legacy." So much so that I concluded that we're "wired" that way.

That makes sense when you consider we're a tribal species. We can't survive for long on our own, so we tribe. The best tribe members contribute; the worst do damage to the tribe and, in less enlightened times and places, are cast out. Nature favors contribution.

Now, survival will always prevail, but survival invites drama. Contribution invites joy.

And it occurs to me that one or the other is always at work beneath the surface, behind the scenes, pulling the strings. See if that rings true for you. Without some "noble cause" aren't you just surviving, just getting by?

What if you never got clear for yourself what contribution or difference you wanted to make in the world? Because there's power in language and clarity, time may be well spent on the question of HOW.

It's not THAT you want to make a difference that makes you special. It's HOW you make a difference that makes you special.

Ask yourself:
What is my life about?
What am I giving my life to?

What if you looked at all your decisions throughout the day, including how to handle the tough situations, and asked, "Am I doing what I'm doing now from a place of survival, or of making a contribution?"

Are you clear on what your contribution is?
Are you honoring that?
How much or how often?

Are you spending too much time and effort surviving?

By the way, surviving can look like fitting in, getting it right, and keeping your nose clean.

Okay, so here are my answers:

My life is about helping people maximize the contribution they make.
I'm giving my life to helping people maximize the contribution they make.

That brings me joy.

It still needs a little polish, but the essence is there.

ELEVATE

ELEVATE

It is not the length of life, but the depth.

Ralph Waldo Emerson

ELEVATE

ELEVATE

What you aim at determines
what you see.

Jordan Peterson

ELEVATE

ELEVATE

Asked of the Dalai Lama, "What has been your favorite moment?"
His reply, "This one."

ELEVATE

ELEVATE

## MAKING PROMISES TO YOURSELF.

Often the most difficult promises to keep are the promises we make to ourselves. Maybe there's a big project that you've been dreaming about that you know would make a big difference in your life your business. Maybe it's sticking to your diet plan or maybe calling back that client that you've been working on but maybe you think they're not interested.

My advice to you is to make a list. Make a list of those items. What have you been promising yourself, but you haven't gotten to it yet? At the beginning of each month take on one of those promises... really take it on and make it happen.

ELEVATE

The purpose of life is not to be happy. It is to be useful, to be honorable, to be compassionate, to have it make some difference that you have lived and lived well.

Ralph Waldo Emerson

ELEVATE

ELEVATE

Conformity is the jailer of freedom and the enemy of growth.

John F. Kennedy

ELEVATE

## STOP MAKING SENSE.

You may think I'm referring to the Talking Heads' concert film.

I'm not.

Consider this instead. When what you say about yourself and your business "makes sense" to others, you lack distinction. You are categorized. You are pigeonholed. You are commoditized, indistinguishable.

That's not what you want. That's not who you are. You are unique. No one offers what you do, in the way that you do.

Rely less on following formulas and utilizing "best practices" to market your business and express your Self, your unique Self.

ELEVATE

To do this you must identify and break down the barriers that stand in the way. You must be willing to be vulnerable and expose yourself.

This may sound risky, but that's the ticket. And it's really not as bad as you think it is.

It's like dancing. You can't be a great dancer by merely knowing the steps. You must free yourself of all constraints and express.

The world will cheer in delight. You are exactly what they've been looking for.

Many wealthy people are little more than janitors of their possessions.

Frank Lloyd Wright

ELEVATE

ELEVATE

## MAKE SURE THE GOOD WOLF WINS.

There's an old Cherokee legend: a grandfather is speaking to his grandson, telling him about life and he says, "Grandson, inside me there's a battle going on between two wolves. One wolf is evil. He represents regret, resentment and anger, The other wolf is good. He represents love and joy and contribution. And that battle is not only going on inside of me, it is going on inside of you and every other person. The grandson asks, "Well, which wolf will win the battle?" The grandfather replies, "Whichever one you feed."

In your business, in your life, there are areas where you are feeding the bad wolf, and areas where you're feeding the good wolf. Get clear on what areas those are, and ask yourself, how can I stop feeding the bad wolf, and start feeding the good wolf even more?

ELEVATE

Security is mostly superstition. It does not exist in nature, nor do the children of men as a whole experience it. Avoiding danger is no safer in the long run than outright exposure. Life is either a daring adventure or nothing.

Helen Keller

ELEVATE

ELEVATE

A leader is best when people
barely know he exists, when his
work is done, his aim fulfilled,
they will say: we did it ourselves.

Lao Tzu

ELEVATE

ELEVATE

The best way to predict the
future is to create it.

Alan Kay

ELEVATE

ELEVATE

Success is the ability to go from one failure to another with no loss of enthusiasm.

Sir Winston Churchill

ELEVATE

ELEVATE

Never doubt that a small group
of thoughtful, committed citizens
can change the world.  Indeed,
it is the only thing that ever has.

Margaret Mead

ELEVATE

ELEVATE

No pessimist ever discovered the secrets of stars, or sailed to an uncharted land, or opened a new heaven to the human spirit.

Helen Keller

ELEVATE

ELEVATE

## YOUR STATE OF HAPPINESS.

Did you know that your level of happiness is determined 50% by your genetics? You're born that way. What's probably more surprising is only 10% is determined by the circumstances and conditions of your life.

But don't we act as if: when I get there…THEN I'll be happy; when I get that promotion…THEN I'll be happy; when the economy recovers…THEN I'll be happy. But it doesn't really work that way. We're born with this set point, our default setting for happiness and it's influenced by the conditions and circumstances, good or bad, but we always return to this sort of set point. So that's 60% of our happiness.

That leaves a whole 40% to deal with. What is that? That's determined by what we're doing and what we are thinking about on a regular basis, on a day-to-day basis. These are the things that bring us happiness, the activities that we enjoy and the things we're thinking about accomplishing and achieving in our lives. That's what we have control over on a regular basis, so as you're moving into the new year, don't think about goal-setting and creating your vision because you're "supposed to" or because you "should" but because these are the things that bring you happiness on a regular basis. By getting back in touch with them you can improve your happiness level anytime you want.

To understand the heart and mind of a person, look not at what he has already achieved, but at what he aspires to.

Kahlil Gibran

ELEVATE

ELEVATE

Far better it is to dare mighty things, to win glorious triumphs, even though checkered by failure, than to take rank with those poor spirits who neither enjoy much nor suffer much, because they live in the gray twilight that knows not victory or defeat.

Theodore Roosevelt

ELEVATE

ELEVATE

When I let go of what I am, I become what I might be. When I let go of what I have, I receive what I need.

Lao Tsu

ELEVATE

ELEVATE

## BE UNCOMFORTABLE...REALLY?

You've probably heard this one before: "To be outstanding, get comfortable being uncomfortable."

Huh? That's like saying "Get happy being depressed." Or, "Life is hard. Get used to suffering."

No thanks.

I understand that significant performance jumps (breakthroughs) may come from doing things that are outside your so-called comfort zone, but do you really shine when you're uncomfortable?

Breakthroughs come from discovering what makes you uncomfortable about the situation and challenging that. The answer isn't "fear," but that can point the way.

The key is not to get outside your comfort zone, but to expand it so you can be more powerful in more situations. A leader is someone who can deal with any situation under any conditions, and not lose their power.

Try it:
Pick a situation that makes you uncomfortable.
Ask, what's the underlying truth about this situation and my relationship to it? Then challenge that truth.
Ask, is this really true?

What would you do if it wasn't?

Do that...unless it's illegal, immoral or unethical, of course.

My life has been filled with terrible misfortune; most of which never happened.

Montaigne

ELEVATE

ELEVATE

This is the true joy in life, being used for a purpose recognized by yourself as a mighty one. Being a force of nature instead of a feverish, selfish little clod of ailments and grievances complaining that the world will not devote itself to making you happy. I am of the opinion that my life belongs to the whole community and as I live it is my privilege - my *privilege* to do for it whatever I can. I want to be thoroughly used up when I die, for the harder I work the more I love. I rejoice in life for its own sake. Life is no brief candle to me; it is a sort of splendid torch which I've got a hold of for the moment and I want to make it burn as brightly as possible before handing it on to future generations.

George Bernard Shaw

ELEVATE

ELEVATE

Man has to suffer. When he has no real afflictions, he invents some.

Jose Marti

ELEVATE

ELEVATE

Great spirits have always encountered violent opposition from mediocre minds.

Albert Einstein

ELEVATE

ELEVATE

In separateness lies the world's great misery; in compassion lies the world's true strength.

Gautama Siddhartha [Buddha]

ELEVATE

ELEVATE

You can have anything you
want in life if you just help
enough other people get what
they want.

Zig Ziglar

ELEVATE

ELEVATE

The key is not to prioritize what's on the schedule, but to schedule your priorities.

Stephen Covey

ELEVATE

ELEVATE

## PERCEPTION IS REALITY. I DON'T THINK SO.

A friend and I recently met for a beer.

I engaged him in a conversation we'd had before around my disdain for the phrase **perception is reality.** My rational mind – I am a trained scientist, after all – tells me that reality is constructed of concrete elements: data, facts, evidence, and the like, with a little conjecture thrown in to fill the voids. Black and white, objective, inarguable, like the effects of gravity, or electricity. Whereas perception is *subjective*. Facts are not required.

This is the logical basis for my assertion that perception and reality do not equate.

Why this matters (to me) is that people too often make decisions without the awareness of this vital distinction and are led astray. In fact, it gets reinforced in our collective consciousness every time its repeated. *You know, if you hear it over and over again, it must be true* (a perception, not a reality). Worse, people in positions of influence and power take advantage of this naivete to build their own personal power without, I fear, the advancement of humanity at heart.

*Wake up.*

So that's a little background about my reality. Or is it my perception about reality? You see, it really is a great concept to explore.

Here's what took it to the next level and had me revisit it with my beer-buddy. I'd recently heard the phrase **perception is more powerful than reality**. I can't argue with that one. It draws a distinction between the two and opens the possibility of consideration, of discerning.

When we mistake our perceptions as reality, we limit what's possible because we've limited the options.

Look for yourself. Where might you be confusing perception with reality, and how are your choices limited by that reality? The truth is, it's all perception. When unquestioned or unchallenged, our options are limited. In business, can you afford to be oblivious to options, to opportunities?

It's your move.

ELEVATE

Finish each day and be done with it. You have done what you could. Some blunders and absurdities no doubt crept in; forget them as soon as you can. Tomorrow is a new day. You shall begin it serenely and with too high a spirit to be encumbered with your old nonsense.

Ralph Waldo Emerson

ELEVATE

ELEVATE

## WHAT WAS THE FIRST PROMISE YOU BROKE TODAY?

Was it when the alarm clock went off?

Wow. Starting the day with a broken promise. Nice.

"What promise? I didn't make a promise," you retort.

Of course you did. You set your alarm, making an agreement with yourself to get up at a certain time.

Then the alarm goes off and the justifications and rationalizations start flowing for why it somehow makes sense to *not* keep your promise.

How "ordinary" of you. Have a nice day.

P.S. Okay, perhaps that was a little harsh. But if you live your life like some promises matter and some promises don't you may be sabotaging yourself and letting others down. You know in your heart you want to serve others, to rise above, and to leave a legacy.

Start your day by keeping your first promise, and then your second: going to the gym, eating a healthy breakfast, etc. See how long you can keep it up. More importantly, notice the difference it makes in your life.

Your task is not to seek for love,
but merely to seek and find all
the barriers within yourself that
you have built against it.

Rumi

ELEVATE

ELEVATE

If you can't describe what you are doing as a process, you don't know what you're doing.

W. Edwards Deming

ELEVATE

ELEVATE

## COUNT YOUR LEMONS.

Behold a lemon. You consider it a sour citrus fruit. But did you also know that it's an insecticide, and a disinfectant, and a battery if you put electrodes in it? It's also a source of revenue for farmers, pickers, packers, truckers, grocers, cashiers, and even for my 10-year-old son who likes to do lemonade stands.

So, what does this have to do with business coaching? Well, we look at a lot of things in our life like they're only one thing – challenges, other people, situations – when in fact there are many other ways to look at what's possible within a particular situation.

Take a look at things in your life that you only see one way, particularly those difficult business challenges and see if you can re-frame them, or look at them in a different way, and see if something else is possible.

ELEVATE

ELEVATE

Your life is the sum result of all the choices you make, both consciously and unconsciously. If you can control the process of choosing, you can take control of all aspects of your life. You can find the freedom that comes from being in charge of yourself.

Robert Foster Bennett

ELEVATE

# CLOSING THOUGHTS.

## SEVEN REASONS YOU NEED A BUSINESS COACH.

No one really, honestly does their best on a challenge when they face it alone. Even if the only help they have is someone cheering them on from the sidelines, that bit of encouragement can make all the difference to overcoming the challenge or succumbing to defeat.

In a business situation, you might not have the luxury of confiding your vision, hopes, fears to one of your staff or even to a family member. At that point, who do you talk to? What happens when faced with the daunting task of firing someone, renovating your goals, or answering the question, "Where do I go from here?"

A business coach can be somewhat like a mentor, or a therapist, or even a treasured confidant. The goal is to find the coach who best suits your personality, can help move you and your dreams forward and will hold you accountable for milestones along the way. So, what does a business coach do, exactly? Here is a list of seven points a good coach should help you with:

1. Provide an objective point of view
2. Provide accountability when setting goals
3. Advocate for your success—help you reach your dreams

ELEVATE

4. Help you expand your comfort zone so you can grow
5. Help you realize the tools and resources you need to be successful
6. Allow you to be authentic with yourself and others
7. Encourage you to stay in action and be unstoppable

1. Provide an objective point of view: Because your coach is not a partner, employee, family member or stake holder in your company and business, he or she can provide a different point of view than the one you are currently getting from your own window, from your employees and other people intricately involved in your business. Your coach doesn't have a financial interest in your company, he has the goal of seeing you succeed.

2. Provide accountability when setting goals: Through regular meetings, whether weekly, monthly or whenever they occur for you, the coach helps you set up action plans to meet the goals the two of you have worked out together. You know you will have to answer to your coach at the next meeting. He's going to ask you if you accomplished the milestone you said you would reach. He's going to want to know if you took the action you said you would. Together you will review your progress and identify what is truly important to you as your values, your mission, your purpose.

3. Advocate for your success: Everyone at some time has set goals only to discover that—whoops—life shows up instead. You experience breakdowns in communication, work efficiency or health. Upsets occur that threaten to spin you off track. A coach

reminds you of your purpose and of who you really are versus the person you sometimes think you are. Having someone objectively say to you, "You can do this" is invaluable. Especially if you have lost sight of the end result. He will also challenge whatever reasons you throw up saying you can't achieve those goals. "Yes, you can," he'll say with confidence.

4. Help expand your comfort zone: Your comfort zone represents the limits of what you know and what you are accustomed to. Another rational voice can bring into your awareness concepts and understandings you might not have ever thought of. There will be areas you might find uncomfortable. A coach helps you explore those areas and even, if appropriate, grow into them.

5. Help you realize the tools and resources you need to be successful: Planning tools and time management is key to stretching your effectiveness in your business. A coach will likely have access to these kinds of tools, to other professionals, and to other key ideas that you might not have known otherwise. You can experience profound paradigm shifts, alternate ways of thinking and new and/or better ways of communicating. Your skills will develop with every encounter.

6. Allow you to be authentic with yourself and others: A coach will call you out on your flakiness and won't take those sorry excuses for not performing. He creates for you a safe, non-judgmental place to be and to grow. This is what allows you to go through the discovery of what is holding you back from realizing your goals, uncovering the fears and objections that

your scared self tells you—the ideas that you can't really make it. Those fears and ideas are blown away in the light of another's rational thinking.

7. Encourage you to stay in action—to be unstoppable: The only reason to not be in action is because you don't have the tools to overcome obstacles. Maybe you don't know what's holding you back, maybe your fear is unwarranted, maybe you need someone to point that out to you. Circumstances will always arise that try to stop you from moving forward. Don't you think it's a good idea to have someone on your side who shines a light in the shadows and helps you move forward? Coaching looks like this: There is usually a preliminary session to lay the groundwork. This might be a one to one meeting, or a classroom situation.

Next, you begin to meet regularly. Maybe it's a two-hour session once a week or a four-hour session every other week. Whatever it is, this is where you become honest with yourself and swallow your pride and fears and really get down to work.

One to one meetings have more flexibility and more intense time spent on working out problems. A classroom's advantage is getting other minds involved in your challenges and finding, maybe, several different approaches to what it is that you want to do.

*This article was written by and published in Business Scene Magazine, January/February 2012 edition. Reprinted with permission.*

# ABOUT THE AUTHOR. JIM MCLAUGHLIN.

Jim's mission is to elevate the conversations in organizations, to have people talking more about what's possible and less about what's wrong.

He stands for a world in which people are connected, compassionate and creative.

His values are reliability, leadership, commitment, compassion, integrity and harmony.

His top five Strength Themes are Responsibility, Learner, Restorative, Communication and Input.

ELEVATE

## Experience

Jim has a diverse background that includes oil exploration, software development, corporate training and performance support, project management and land development.

## Education

He received a Master of Business Administration degree from San Diego State University, a Bachelor of Science degree from the University of the Pacific and did post-graduate work at California State University Northridge and Los Angeles.

## Community

Jim is an active member of Toastmasters International, a leader in Scouting, a Rotarian, board member of the Economic Development Coalition of Southwest Riverside County (California), and organizer of TEDx Temecula, a locally organized TED event, now in its eighth year.

ELEVATE

ELEVATE

# JIM'S SERVICES.

## EXECUTIVE COACHING.

As an executive, you need an edge: to stay ahead of the competition, to stay ahead of the market, and to stay ahead of the breakdowns that show up inside your organization.

My one-on-one Executive Coaching programs provide the flexibility you need and are customized to your unique business environment.

## MANAGEMENT CONSULTING.

Your organization is a network of conversations that pass up and down the management chain. It's critical that these conversations be effective.

ELEVATE

Often, they are not.

Our programs turn managers into leaders, whether they are new to their positions, or they have been in management for much of their careers.

## SALES PERFORMANCE.

Successful sales begin with developing a powerful connection with the prospect. When we are disconnected, we are separate, and the prospect feels it. You've probably felt it yourself.

Most sales training is motivational and falls short because it does not stick. Our sales programs are not motivational or traditional. They are transformational and alter the salesperson's relationship to sales. The benefits of transformational programs last.

# CONTACT THE AUTHOR.

jim@effectiveactionconsulting.com

jim@jamesrmclaughlin.com

Twitter @jimmclaughlin

FB: @YourObiWan

LinkedIn.com/in/WorkWithJim/

Jim McLaughlin | 951-225-2179

ELEVATE

Made in the USA
Lexington, KY
09 December 2019

58354479R00066